HELLO, BODY! LUNGS

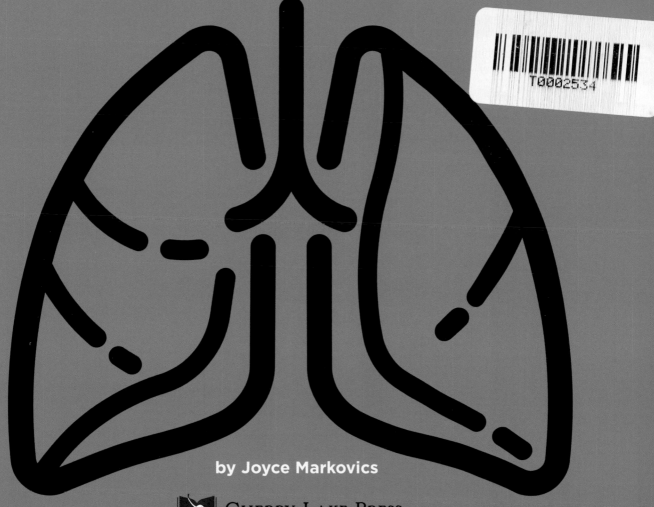

by Joyce Markovics

CHERRY LAKE PRESS
Ann Arbor, Michigan

Published in the United States of America by Cherry Lake Publishing Group
Ann Arbor, Michigan
www.cherrylakepublishing.com

Reading Adviser: Beth Walker Gambro, MS Ed., Reading Consultant, Yorkville, IL
Content Advisers: Sharon Markovics, MD, and Peter Markovics, MD
Book Designer: Ed Morgan

Photo Credits: Courtesy of Farm Security Administration - Office of War Information Photograph Collection (Library of Congress), 4; Courtesy of Library of Congress, 5; © Paul Alexander; CDC/Wikimedia Commons, 7; freepik.com, 8–9; freepik.com, 10; freepik.com, 11; freepik.com, 12; © Javier Regueiro/Shutterstock, 13; © Aldona Griskeviciene/ Shutterstock, 15; freepik.com, 15; freepik.com, 16; © crystal light/Shutterstock, 17; freepik.com, 18; © mi_viri/ Shutterstock, 19; freepik.com, 20; © Billion Photos/Shutterstock, 21.

Cherry Lake Press is an imprint of Cherry Lake Publishing Group.

Library of Congress Cataloging-in-Publication Data

Names: Markovics, Joyce L., author.
Title: Lungs / by Joyce Markovics.
Description: Ann Arbor, Michigan : Cherry Lake Publishing, [2023] | Series:
  Hello, body! | Includes bibliographical references and index. |
  Audience: Grades 4-6
Identifiers: LCCN 2022003835 (print) | LCCN 2022003836 (ebook) | ISBN
  9781668909621 (hardcover) | ISBN 9781668911228 (paperback) | ISBN
  9781668914403 (pdf) | ISBN 9781668912812 (ebook)
Subjects: LCSH: Lungs—Juvenile literature.
Classification: LCC QP121 M349 2023 (print) | LCC QP121 (ebook) | DDC
  612.2/4—dc23/eng/20220330
LC record available at https://lccn.loc.gov/2022003835
LC ebook record available at https://lccn.loc.gov/2022003836

Printed in the United States of America by
Corporate Graphics

CONTENTS

IRON LUNG

It was a hot summer day in Texas in 1952. Six-year-old Paul Alexander was playing outside when he began to feel sick. He had a headache, stiff neck, and fever. Paul rushed inside to tell his mom. Days later, the little boy couldn't move. Paul had polio, a deadly **virus** that can cause **paralysis**.

In Paul's case, the virus also made it hard for him to speak, swallow, and even breathe. Paul was gasping for air. To help Paul breathe, doctors put him in an iron lung, a kind of **ventilator**. The iron lung saved his life.

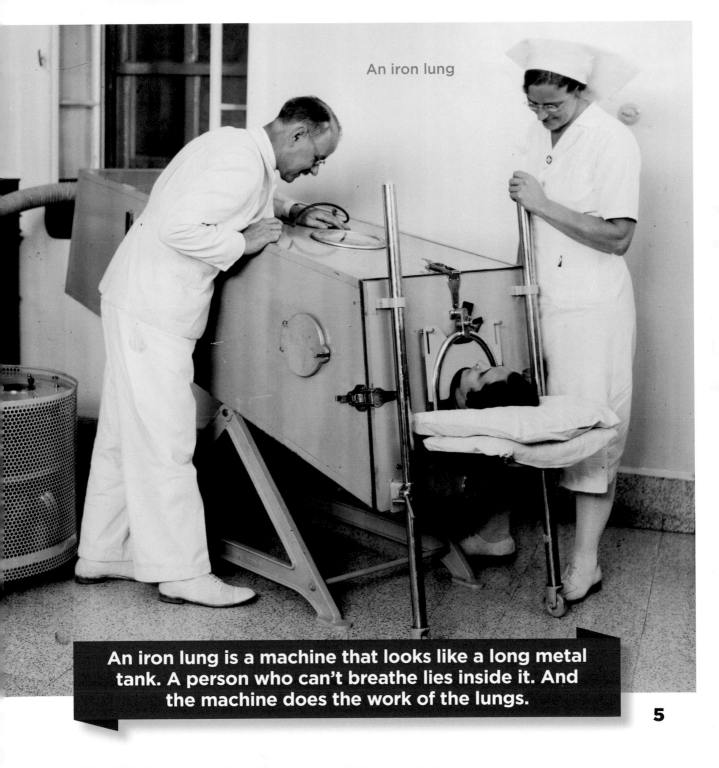

An iron lung

An iron lung is a machine that looks like a long metal tank. A person who can't breathe lies inside it. And the machine does the work of the lungs.

 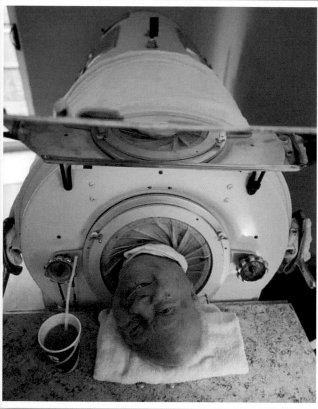

"Living is so amazing to me," said Paul Alexander, who's shown here in his iron lung as a child and as an adult.

More than 70 years later, an iron lung is still keeping Paul alive. When he was younger, he was able to breathe outside of the machine for short periods. But today, he lives inside it.

Despite his struggles, Paul earned college and law degrees. He even wrote a book about his life. When others told Paul he couldn't do something, he said, "Oh yes I can!" Paul added, "My story is an example of why your past or even **disability** does not have to define your future."

This 1963 poster encourages people to get the polio vaccine, which was given by mouth at the time.

In 1955, a polio vaccine became available. Thanks to the vaccine, the disease was eradicated in the United States. At its peak, polio affected over half a million people per year.

A LOOK AT THE LUNGS

Breathe in! Do you feel your chest get a little bigger? That's your two lungs at work. They fill up most of your chest. Now touch your chest. You can probably feel your hard ribs. Your lungs are protected by 12 pairs of them. They form your rib cage.

At the base of your ribs and beneath your lungs is a stretchy dome-shaped muscle. It's called a diaphragm (DY-uh-fram). It works together with your lungs so you can breathe in, or inhale, and breathe out, or exhale.

Human lungs and diaphragm

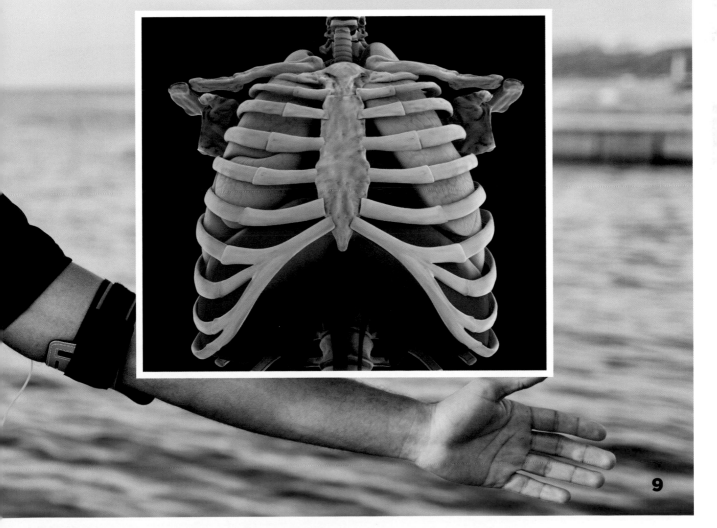

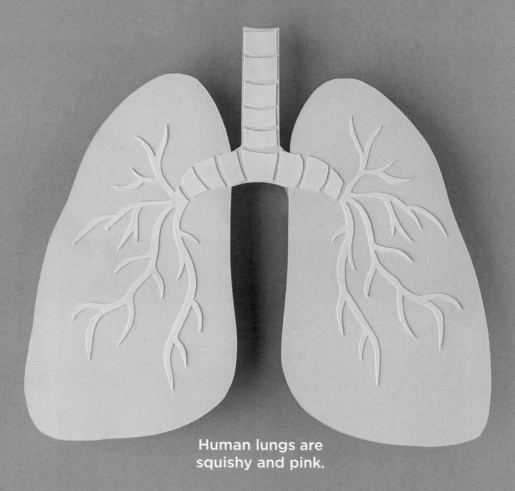

Human lungs are
squishy and pink.

Your lungs are a key part of the respiratory (REH-spruh-taw-ree) system. You wouldn't be able to breathe without this **vital** system. As we inhale, it brings fresh air into our lungs. Fresh air contains oxygen, which our bodies and cells need. When we exhale, the respiratory system helps us release **carbon dioxide**.

Our respiratory system also allows us to talk! This system includes your nose, mouth, throat, voice box, windpipe, and lungs. All of these body parts work together to keep you breathing—and talking.

The act of breathing is called respiration (reh-spuh-RAY-shuhn).

BREATHE IN AND OUT

Breathing involves a lot of steps. First, air enters your respiratory system through your nose or mouth. If you breathe through your nose, tiny hairs, or cilia (SIH-lee-uh), filter the air. They trap dust and other small particles. Your nifty nose also warms and moistens the air as you breathe it in!

Then the air enters your throat. Deep in the throat is where the **pharynx** is located and the pathway divides in two. One tube called the esophagus (ih-SAH-fuh-gus) carries food to the stomach. The other tube carries air to your lungs.

pharynx

epiglottis

esophagus

Parts of the upper respiratory system

A flap of tissue—the epiglottis (eh-puh-GLAH-tuhs)—stops food and liquid from going into the lungs when you swallow.

At the top of the air-only tube is your voice box, or larynx (LAR-ingks). Without it, you wouldn't be able to talk, laugh, yell, or sing! This hollow body part holds your vocal cords. They open, close, and **vibrate** to make sounds.

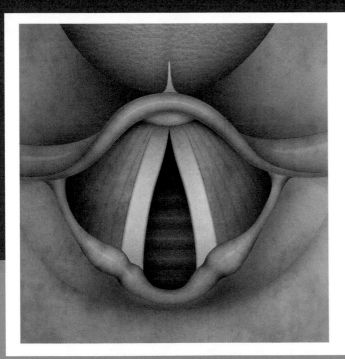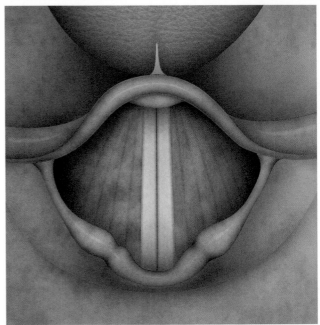

Opened and closed vocal cords

How much air you breathe into your lungs affects how loud and long you can talk. For example, shouting or singing requires a lot of air. Try singing one of your favorite songs. How far can you get without taking a breath? Not that far, right?

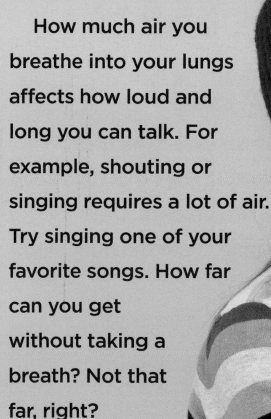

A hiccup happens when your diaphragm doesn't work right and causes you to suck in air. When the fast-moving air hits your voice box, your vocal cords close suddenly. *Hiccup!*

AMAZING ALVEOLI

Below the larynx is your windpipe. It's also called the trachea (TRAY-kee-uh). The windpipe is lined with stiff rings that help keep it open. At the bottom of the trachea are two **bronchi**. One connects to the left lung, and the other connects to the right lung.

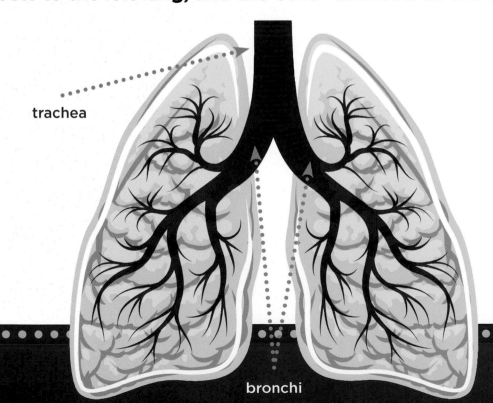

trachea

bronchi

Here's what your alveoli would look like under a powerful microscope.

The bronchi divide into smaller and smaller tubes much like the branches on a tree. The thinnest ones are about as thick as a human hair! At the end of each tiny tube is a clump of very tiny air sacs. These are your alveoli (al-VEE-uh-lye).

Inside your lungs are about 600 million alveoli. In fact, if you stretched them out, they would cover an entire tennis court! Each one is wrapped in teensy blood vessels, or capillaries. When you breathe in, the alveoli fill with air like mini balloons.

This is where the exchange of oxygen and carbon dioxide takes place. Oxygen moves from the alveoli into the blood through the capillaries. At the same time, carbon dioxide moves out of the blood and into the alveoli to be exhaled. The oxygen-rich blood then travels to your entire body!

As you inhale, your diaphragm moves down so your lungs can fill with air. When you exhale, it moves up to help push air out of your lungs.

LUNG DISORDERS

Lung problems can make breathing hard. Asthma (AZ-muh) occurs when the airways in the lungs swell up and fill with **mucus**. Then air can't pass as easily and breathing gets harder. The good news is there are lots of medicines to treat asthma.

Most asthma medicine is breathed into the lungs using an inhaler.

COPD is another lung disease that makes it hard to breathe. However, it can be prevented. COPD is almost always caused by smoking. So do your lungs a favor, and don't smoke!

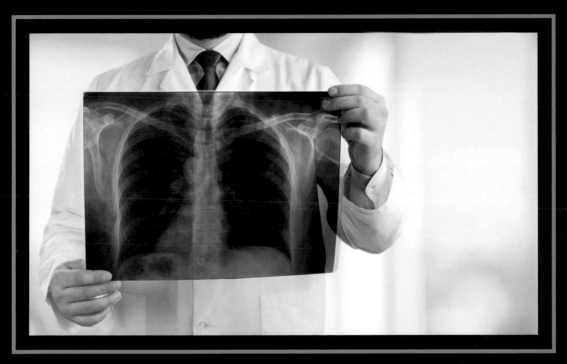

COPD stands for chronic obstructive pulmonary disease.

Pneumonia is a lung infection caused by viruses or bacteria. It affects more than 5 million people each year.

HEALTH TIPS

Here are some ways to keep your lungs healthy:

- Don't smoke! This is one of the best ways to keep your lungs healthy.

- Keep your lungs strong by exercising at least three times a week. Walk, play, bike, jump, or dance.

- Eat lots of healthy foods, such as vegetables, fruits, and whole grains. And avoid sugary drinks such as soda and fruit juice.

GLOSSARY

bacteria (bac-TIHR-ee-uh) tiny living things; some bacteria are useful, while others can cause disease

bronchi (BRONG-kee) the two main branches of the trachea

capillaries (KAH-puh-lehr-eez) tiny blood vessels

carbon dioxide (KAR-buhn dye-OK-side) a gas that is a combination of carbon and oxygen; it is released when things break down

disability (diss-uh-BIH-luh-tee) a condition of the body that can make it hard to do certain things

eradicated (ih-rah-duh-KAY-tuhd) gotten rid of something completely

infection (in-FEK-shuhn) an illness caused by germs

mucus (MYOO-kuhss) a sticky liquid made by the body

paralysis (puh-RAL-uh-siss) the inability to move or feel a part or parts of one's body

pharynx (FEHR-ingks) the tube that connects the mouth and nose with the esophagus

pneumonia (noo-MOH-nyuh) a disease of the lungs that makes it difficult to breathe

tissue (TISH-oo) a group of similar cells that form a part of or an organ in the body

vaccine (vak-SEEN) a medicine that protects a person from a particular disease

ventilator (VEN-tuh-lay-tuhr) equipment that moves air into and out of a person's lungs

vibrate (VYE-brayt) to move up and down or back and forth quickly

virus (VYE-ruhss) a tiny germ that can invade cells and cause disease

vital (VYE-tuhl) very important

FIND OUT MORE

BOOKS

Figorito, Christine. *The Lungs in Your Body*. New York, NY: Rosen Publishing Group, 2015.

Simon, Seymour. *The Human Body*. New York, NY: HarperCollins, 2008.

Simon, Seymour. *Lungs: Your Respiratory System*. New York, NY: HarperCollins, 2007.

WEBSITES

National Museum of Health and Medicine: Respiratory System
https://www.medicalmuseum.mil/index.cfm?p=visit.exhibits.past.visiblyhuman.page_03

Science Museum: The Iron Lung
https://www.sciencemuseum.org.uk/objects-and-stories/medicine/iron-lung

Science Museum of Minnesota: The Lungs
https://www.smm.org/heart/lungs/top.html

INDEX

ABOUT THE AUTHOR

Joyce Markovics has written hundreds of books for kids. She would like to thank Sharon—a lover of lungs—for her decades of work as an amazing allergist and for her expertise in reviewing this and the other books in this series.